READING POWER

Nature's Greatest Hits

Greenland
World's Largest Island

Joanne Mattern

The Rosen Publishing Group's
PowerKids Press™
New York

Published in 2002 by The Rosen Publishing Group, Inc.
29 East 21st Street, New York, NY 10010

First Edition

Book Design: Michael DeLisio

Photo Credits: Cover, pp. 8–9 © Robert Estall/Corbis; pp. 4–5, 9 (inset), 10–11, 18–19 © Indexstock; pp. 12–13 © Layne Kennedy/Corbis; p. 13 (inset) © Dan Guravich/Corbis; pp. 14–15, 19 (inset) © Wolfgang Kaehler/Corbis; p. 14 (inset) © National Geographic; p. 15 (inset) © Paul A. Souders/Corbis; p. 16 (top), 16 (bottom) © Michael Lewis/Corbis; pp. 20–21 © Hubert Stadler/Corbis

Mattern, Joanne, 1963–
Greenland : world's largest island / Joanne Mattern.
  p. cm. — (Nature's greatest hits)
Includes bibliographical references (p.   ).
ISBN 0-8239-6018-8 (lib. bdg.)
1. Greenland—Juvenile literature. [1. Greenland.]   I. Title. II. Series.
CURR G743 .M38 2001 2002
998'.2—dc21

2001000595

Manufactured in the United States of America

Contents

World's Largest Island

An island is land that has water on all sides. The world's largest island is Greenland. It has an area of about 840,000 square miles.

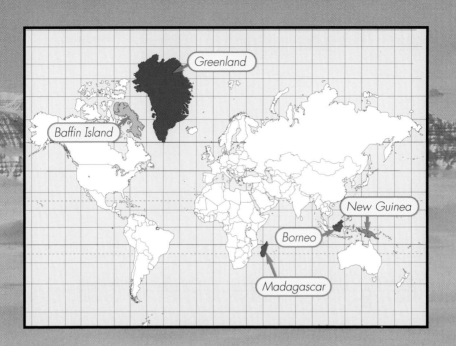

The World's Largest Islands

Name	Square Miles
Greenland	840,000 miles
New Guinea	310,000 miles
Borneo	290,000 miles
Madagascar	226,658 miles
Baffin Island, Canada	195,928 miles

Greenland is in the Atlantic and Arctic Oceans. It is close to Canada. One part of Greenland is only ten miles away from Canada.

North
Pole

Arctic Ocean

Greenland

Atlantic Ocean

Canada

United States

7

Most of Greenland is covered by a large ice sheet. Much of the ice is 5,000 feet deep. In some places, it is about 10,000 feet deep.

IT'S A FACT: The ice on Greenland holds ten percent of the world's fresh water.

Weather

It is very cold in Greenland. In winter, the temperature may go as low as −90 degrees Fahrenheit. In summer, the temperature may reach only 50 degrees Fahrenheit.

IT'S A FACT: The Vikings named
this cold, icy island "Greenland"
to get people to go and live there.

Animals

The animals that live in Greenland are used to the cold weather. Animals such as polar bears and reindeer have thick fur that keeps them warm. The dogs that live in Greenland have thick fur, too. They help people by pulling heavy sleds over miles of ice.

IT'S A FACT: The world's largest national park is in Greenland. It is called the Northeast Greenland National Park. It is bigger than England and France put together!

Blue whale

Many animals live in the waters around Greenland. Seals and walruses eat the fish. Blue whales, Greenland whales, and many other kinds of whales live near Greenland, too.

Walruses stay together on the rocks near the shore.

About two million seals live in Greenland's waters.

People

Only about 55,000 people live
in Greenland. Most people who
live in Greenland were born there.

Country	Number of People
Greenland	55,000
Denmark	5,336,000
United States	276,000,000

Denmark

The country of Denmark owns the island of Greenland.

IT'S A FACT: There are no roads between towns in Greenland. People must sail or fly to get from one town to another.

Water is a very important part of people's lives in Greenland. Most people live near the water. Many people in Greenland fish for a living.

The kayak was first made in Greenland.

Visiting Greenland

Although it is cold and icy, more than 16,000 people visit Greenland every year. Some visitors even stay in a hotel made out of ice!

There are many interesting things to see in Greenland, the world's largest island.

Glossary

Fahrenheit (**far**-uhn-hyt) a way of measuring temperature with 32 degrees being the temperature at which water freezes

island (**eye**-luhnd) a piece of land with water on all sides

kayak (**ky**-ak) a lightweight canoe with a small opening in the middle to sit in

temperature (**tehm**-puhr-uh-chuhr) how hot or cold something is

Vikings (**vy**-kihngz) sailors who lived long ago who were great warriors and explorers

Resources

Books
People of the Polar Regions
by Jen Green
Raintree Steck-Vaughn (1998)

The Arctic Land
by Bobbie Kalman
Econo-Clad Books (1999)

Web Site
Greenland Crossing
http://www.greenlandcrossing.com/
   kid-en/index-ke.htm

Index

Word Count: 340

Note to Librarians, Teachers, and Parents

If reading is a challenge, Reading Power is a solution! Reading Power is perfect for readers who want high-interest subject matter at an accessible reading level. These fact-filled, photo-illustrated books are designed for readers who want straightforward vocabulary, engaging topics, and a manageable reading experience. With clear picture/text correspondence, leveled Reading Power books put the reader in charge. Now readers have the power to get the information they want and the skills they need in a user-friendly format.